Coffee and Cream

Dr. Bronzie Dabney

Illustrated by Ervin A. Sims

Archway Publishing books may be ordered through booksellers or by contacting:

Archway Publishing
1663 Liberty Drive
Bloomington, IN 47403
www.archwaypublishing.com
844-669-3957

Because of the dynamic nature of the Internet, any web addresses or links contained in this book may have changed since publication and may no longer be valid. The views expressed in this work are solely those of the author and do not necessarily reflect the views of the publisher, and the publisher hereby disclaims any responsibility for them.

Any people depicted in stock imagery provided by Getty Images are models, and such images are being used for illustrative purposes only.
Certain stock imagery © Getty Images.

Interior Image Credit: Ervin A. Sims

ISBN: 978-1-6657-3214-7 (sc)
ISBN: 978-1-6657-3215-4 (e)

Print information available on the last page.

Archway Publishing rev. date: 10/19/2022

Dedicated to

Aiden James Dabney

with love

♥

Special acknowledgement to Patricia E. Robinson who shared her coffee & cream experience

I look a little different than
most of my friends.

My hair and skin color
are not like theirs.

But that is alright
with me,
I don't care!

We got off the bus and started walking. My friend stopped me and whispered a question in my ear,

"what race are you"?

Still, at the end of the day
when I went home,
I too began to wonder, "what race am I?"
The question was stuck in my head.

I kept thinking and thinking about what I could have said.

No answer yet...I decided to just go to bed.

After I fell asleep I had a dream
about coffee and cream.
The dream was an answer
to my riddle.

My one parent is brown

like coffee

and my other parent

is the color of cream

and I am in the middle.

I know who I am
and where I come from.
That is important
for a child to know.

I also know that
I am loved
because love is what
helps me grow.

Each person is different.

Each person is unique.

I see differences

every day of the week.

I am learning
to accept people for who they are
to keep from strife.

People are special.
What makes that nice?
Everyone has a purpose in life.

asian   australoid   black   white

23

If anyone else were to ask me,

"what race are you?"

I will not be at a loss for words.

I am the best of two races AND

my answer is sensational.

I am proud to be

bi-racial.

My hair may be curly or straight
and I may have a brown
or cream colored face.

But most important
in this case is,
I am a part of the human race!

Note to Parents

A bi-racial identity could be both confusing and challenging to a young child as they try to understand where they fit into society. As an educator, as well as a parent, I observed how children thrive when they realize they are not alone in their experience. Reading about someone else who is going through the same or similar situation can give a young person self-assurance.

This Bibliotherapy book can be used to spark a conversation about defining and recognizing racial differences. The talk may not be easy but will help young children better understand their bi-racial heritage. Additionally, it could provide them with self-confidence and coping skills.

Questions and Answers to consider about a bi-racial/multi-racial identity: Q: How many races are there in the world?

A: The world population is divided into four major races: Asian/Mongoloid, Australoid, Black/Negroid, and White/Caucasian. However, there are over 5,000 ethnicities.

Q: What is the right age to begin to talk about Race?

A: Experts claim that children notice differences in apperance and race as young as three years old. Therefore, don't delay the conversation about race. Talk honestly and openly about it so you can empower your little ones.

Q: The most commonly asked question is, "What Are You?"

A: Teach your children about diversity. Specifically, explain the heritage of each parent. Make it plain to them who they are.

Q: What are your true feelings about racial groups other than your own?

A: Children will pick up on this and follow suit. So, if you want them to value diversity, be a role model.

Help your children to learn to love who they are and to value their differences. The final outcome should be that they will feel secure knowing that the races of both parents play an equally important role in their identity.

Disclaimer

The information within this book reflects the author's personal opinion and experience. It is not intented to take the place of a qualified, licensed family therapist. Research shows that children adjust positively with the help of professional intervention.

Dr. Bronzie Dabney is a member of the
Society of Children's Book Writers and Illustrators (SCBWI)

Inspired by this family:

Alicia, Aiden & Brian

This excellent picture book was written to lovingly explain a bi-racial identity to a young child using colorful illustrations and cheerful rhymes. The character in this book learns a valuable lesson about who he is and learns how to answer the common question, "What Are You?" Parents and children will love reading this book over and over again!

Dr. Bronzie Dabney, educator and author along with her son illustrator Brian J. Dabney create Bibliotherapy picture books for early childhood and elementary age children to help them better understand the circumstances and situations they may encounter resulting from adult life choices.

Look for Dr. Dabney's Modern Family Children's Book Series on topics about Adoption/Foster Care, Bullying, Diversity, Divorce, Living with a Disability/Disabled Family Member, Manners, Moving, Non-traditional families, Serious Illness and others.

A Book for All Ages and Races

Printed in the United States
by Baker & Taylor Publisher Services